EXQUISITE CORPSE

Malú Urriola

Translated by Elena Barcia

This is a work of poetry. The people, memories, facts, places, and ideas in this books are from the creative mind of the author, and are entirely fictional.

Attention schools and businesses: for discounted copies on large orders, please contact the publisher directly.

For information contact:
Unsolicited Press
Portland, Oregon
www.unsolicitedpress.com
orders@unsolicitedpress.com
619-354-8005

Editor: Summer Stewart
Cover Designer: Katie McCann

ISBN-13:978-1-963115-41-3

He sits at the table and writes
"With this poem you will not seize power," he says.
"With these verses you will not create the Revolution," he says.
"Even with thousands of verses you will not create the Revolution," he says.

Juan Gelmán

If as a matter of fact, it is a clear night
I would say almost relentlessly clear.
Anne Carson

Poetry, you're back!
The wait has been miserable.

I've staggered through life senselessly.
Paths without you are not paths.

Skies become deaf.

Stones don't shine,
nor are the irises of the security cameras
a different color.
Nor does the night perfume the air,
nor does the sun dazzle, nor do doors give shelter.

It's all a mad coming and going,
a waste of larval time,
a clamor of life,
a gate without rivers,
a stormy absence,
an aimless fog,
a star
floating
inside a lightbulb.

The plum trees surrender to the blizzard, shedding
hundreds of petals the wind sweeps along the ground
to show these miserable eyes the transience of being.

Those who seconds ago trembled at the onset of the breeze
are now crawling.

The thing about poetry, it's all about the beginning
and the end.

I'm writing a book that seems to be.

That begins to flow like a river,
like a new branch
of a plant growing imperceptibly in your house,
a leaf falling from a tree,
a cadaver on a slab in the morgue,
a bag floating in emptiness.
I say emptiness to name a town of buildings,
of cables, of windows,
of desolate antennas,
of clothing and fences
where no one knows anybody.

I say emptiness as one says infinite,
like the end of the world.
I say I would do anything to be able to read this book
and to know what it means *to be*.

I say this to you like a cactus
on the road of the soul,
covered in long spines.
I say this to you with a flower,
red and wild, for a crown,
that you could only take without touching me.
For you to exist, there must be an outside
and I am all inside.

While Billie Holiday sings "Take All of Me" with the rhythm of madness entering an empty house, I remembered another night and another house, where words like spores of light disperse, scattering like the memory of savagery, like the protests when thugs try to emulate rain to drive people away, only they are acidic, much like what stairs taste when they lick the sole of a shoe. Death is watching them too, but they don't seem to know it.

Did you know that we are traveling
on a shooting star?

That's why we are so afraid of death.

Mama! Picasso!

Creationism i$ Death

Pigeons peck at the seeds of this old acacia.

Children oblivious to the nightmare of humanity
swing to and fro in the paradise of cruelty.

On the bench facing me, a couple kisses with the voracity
of people who are going to lose themselves.

They wipe their lips at the same time, with the same hand,
the same gesture, as those who are already lost.

She says: It's good-bye. And her eyes begin to leave.
She gathers her coat and departs, just as the future flees
without looking back.

He's staring at a few seeds from the old acacia,
oblivious to the meaning of detachment.

The woman from the bench crosses paths with an elderly lady
in a wheelchair, pushed by an immaculate nurse
with a white cap and white stockings, there where a boy's ball
is bouncing, while his mother yanks on his ear.

The nurse bends down to examine her ankle
and stares into my eyes.
I have a scar like the Southern Cross that shines for me,

I tell her, from my eye to my mouth.
But the nurse lifts her aseptic eyes and looks ahead.

With the coolness of a healthcare worker, her hands grip
the handles and she pushes the old woman who fixes her gaze
on the pigeons taking flight. And soaring just like that
is how things in this life depart.

I have a thirst for winds that batter the ribs,
the intestines, the eyes, the cups, the dishes, the bed.

I let it go. I let it become a distant dot that will
eventually disappear, the way almost all the things
we once loved vanish…and other things that we
will never know.

Passion has always filled my house with flowers.
I say passion as others say wind.

Do you remember *Sexys Bar?*
And that drag queen at the *El Barón* imitating Juan Gabriel
and the misogynist poet talking about his anthology that
with any luck, will be read by the woman who supports him.

It's hot and my body remembers the poem by Constantine
as the scent emerges from a small bouquet of gardenias
that a child, exploited by all of us, sells this hot and humid night in
Guadalajara, Mexico, in room 607 of the Fénix Hotel when Juan
Gabriel stops singing *sweetheart.*

There are two cardinal points = The South

Poetry is not a little woman waiting for a few pats on
her behind, nor is it the canticles of loud-mouthed alcoholics
whose pathetic images could never eclipse Wilms Montt,
or the pederast verses they sing to the miniskirts of young
girls, or their harrowing cries for a world that forgot them
in a bar.

Nor are they more innovative because they're more obscene,
nor more performable because they're more naked.
Certainly,
the more misogynist, the more servile,
and the more learned, the more docile.

The I against life
has been futilely ripped open *ad nauseum.*

The future happens unforeseeably.
No control
over past events or those to come
on the path of *poiesis.*

If you don't acquire the glory of an elite sadder than
a thousand mutes, do not mire your verses in things
that will turn yellow.

The essence of poetry is emanation.
If a star becomes distracted, it takes its own life.

A poet recited into the ear of the night that he was
the word empty.

He enunciated the first person "I" instead of the words ocean, fish,
flight...sky...other, haiku, Larism, baroque,
and a sea of things that exist where nothing yet exists.

What has been loved returns, and what has ceased being loved
is remembered the way a dog licks a scar even though
many years have passed.

Like a quadriplegic, you replay every one of the nights
you have loved.
Like an animal, you remember the taste, the perfume that sated
you, and then you remember death licking your mouth with its
withered lips.

¿What the hell, exactly, do we know about life?

So little. But we love it.

Butterflies are the memory of beauty.

vita brevis...arte longis...

If an otter were to look at itself in the mirror,
it would see what I see:
The reflection of an otter not suitable for pedants
or beautiful geniuses.

Although it longs for the river, the otter delights in the caged
pool, the way a dog delights in barking at the waves.

Dogs are seduced by things that are impossible.

That's why I might also see a dog in the mirror
with the uncertainty of being no more than the dust
of a dog standing upright on two legs.

The epistle of a stormy tragicomic self
that relentlessly extolls
the training of muscles for an ephemeral life.

After a few glasses of wine,
and this vague sensation of floundering
from one day to the next, we paid the check and left the bar.

The moon had the sardonic smile of Carrol's cat.

When we got into her car, she asked: Where are we going?

To the same Dantesque inferno, I thought, but I responded
with another question.
So after talking about her boss, and mine, and about
the overtime gifted to the pockets of other acacias – that
were beginning to burst yellow in those dead streets of
the affluent neighborhood, gated with electricity –
we allowed the silhouette of the mountains reclining
against the night to hang, in the middle of our mouths,
a thirst impossible to quench.

And at intervals we slept and we returned to our infernal kissing
until daybreak.

I pretended to sleep until she awoke, or pretended to wake,
and then – as if she were going to say that forbidden
word, negotiated in the terror of silence – she said, I hope González
wins.

When I arrived at my house, the man sweeping the street told me that González had won the bronze medal.

Since that sunny morning, I never learned what the hell became of her, nor who the fuck was González.

Behind that beautiful poster offering you a life of dreams hides the worst nightmare of all.

It would be better for us to be stepped on by an

I open my eyes and there's that sound murmuring on the back of
my neck like a song that doesn't stop, but when it does, it quivers.

I dream and when I dream, others live inside me. And I dwell in
another house, a house I don't know and that I should begin to
memorize as I venture deeper inside.
The house has stairs, but I ignore where they lead.

My life is divided according to the materials that have
come into my hands, first there were the old bones of
a tree, the powder from a butterfly's wings, the spores of dust in the
light.

I don't even write to earn a living.

Reading is a crime, like stealing in a supermarket. They will send
you to hell and take advantage of the fact that you are less than
nothing to satisfy their greed for everything.

A window. Sometimes I would like a window to look backwards,
to see so many prayers in the stars, some fading in silence,
the way the eyes of drones expire.

Lyrical I, there you are,
greeting the old banners
of a party whose teeth were smashed by the Right
and then ordered they be replaced in gold.

Before leaving to drop off the car at your house,
climbing up four flights of stairs for a sip of water
that you will give me to drink from your mouth.

On a night like this, our asses got so lit
we moaned like an old dresser on the edge of the abyss.

Of that, only the memory that drops by some afternoons
and the pistil of this air flower ground into blue powder
between my fingers.

Never forget even for one day that death will be the last one to kiss my lips.

Things age, my dear Melville,
increasingly fewer worries disturb this erratic peace.

Seagulls settle on the sand to contemplate the ocean
which is their business, what they know and live by.

And the waves with their yoyo of waves break
Narcissus-like on the shore. I'm staying, I'm leaving.

A cloud barely dares to graze the ocean.
And a green ray of lightning turns us on and off.

The firmament is determined to shine – with the fervor of a minor literary critic of a right-wing tabloid – perfecting a shimmer more powerful than the best poetic truth.

By the way…

Let's cast 100% doubt on all good ideas.

A good idea is scary BS that will be endorsed by
much younger fish.

As for us and the Lyrical I, we cannot imagine another future
beyond that wave that, trying to reach the clouds,
falls exhausted by the sand.

THERE
WAS
LIGHTNING
INVOLVED

NO
MATTER
WHAT
THEY
SAY

THERE
WAS
LIGHT
NI
N
G

Ah, memories, they come all this way and make papers fly,
make words fail,
make them insignificant tonight,
make them flatten mountains darker than the sky.

The wing of a satellite falls, and before scorching
the afternoon's torso, it flies incandescent,
like the overwhelming feeling in these bones that,
one way or another, death has already defeated me.

A wind field sways in the poplars, the way your eyes
looked at me when you told me, casually, that Di Giorgio
didn't love anyone.

Except poetry – I thought – except poetry.

Remember when you showed me
The Compact Oxford English Dictionary
you had to read with a magnifying glass?

It was close to 11:00 in Buenos Aires,
the warm air made the jasmine speak.
You read me Juana Bignozzi, and we went
to a place where a guy blended vodka with bananas
and ice beneath the phosphorescent halo of the bar.

In the reprise of a bad imitation of Lynch,
an ambiguous young woman,
her eyes glazed,
sang "Waiting for a Miracle."

We returned to your house, to the *Oxford English Dictionary*, and I
fell asleep in your arms.

Now I'm leaving in a taxi through Pueyrredón
on my way to a country where poets despise each other.

Umbrellas live to lick the rain.
Poets, life.

To live, you have to have bones
that aren't afraid of becoming dust.

STARS LIGHT UP THE SOUTHERN
SKY
NIGHT
A CONSONAN
MISPLACE   DISORIENT
STUNNE
EXCITE
STUFFE
OVERSHADOWE
REVOLUTIONIZE
SADDENE
UNABL
TO LOS
COMPOSUR
LIK A
PROPELE
THT
CUT
THE
AI

It grows dark over the Pacific.

The wind and the clouds have woven a pink shawl.
The pelicans glide over the ocean
and fly away, their craws brimming with fish
the nets were not able to drag in,
this dusk in which the sun abandons us
to our fate, with no evening stars.

While you yearn for that love you deserted
I, in your arms, yearn for that love too cowardly to have me.

Lola Mora

The moon lunating the night cools the days' fever.

It harnesses the tides, awakens the beasts' bad temper.

We were guilty of atoning for hell and created miracles
to see god.

Spinning as usual, time bent its gaze toward our eyes.

And blind, we tried to see the sun.

That's why it hurts, you have to close your eyes.

Who is out there? Who?

Who is there, inside?

In the pupils of a cat's eyes you can see the ocean

and the moon.

An astral body, but green

like an acrobat dancing on the tightrope of outer space

and falling, falling, falling

into the velvet bottom of a box of stars

without light, or strength, or desire.

Falling because travelers have an urge to fall

and rising again because it's an eternal cosmonaut

because the sky belongs to it

and the water.

A butterfly dances in the middle of our soul.

Our wild boar of a body races around the world

searching for food.

Our condor wings fly grazing the mountains

from west to west.

You were telling me about Lola Mora?

(Poem written with four hands with Celeste Carballo)

2 mole men dig in the middle of the asphalt where months
later, they will dig again.

We walk surrounded by traffic, horns, buildings
crying their building tears. Close to the Rex Theatre,
a Japanese woman smiles at us, while red lights glide
under her lips forming for our eyes the word Toyota.

THE POET IS A VISIONARY
ROMANTICS ALWAYS

THE POET IS A CRAFTSMAN OF THE WORD
PARNASSIANS UNITED

THE WORLD IS A MYSTERY & POETRY IS MUSIC
AVANT GARDE SYMBOLISTS

ILLUSION OF PROGRESS & DISASSOCIATION FROM
BOURGEOIS SOCIETY THROUGH ART
WOKE MODERNISTS

THE POET SEEKS TRUTH ABOVE BEAUTY
GENERATION OF '98

THE POET IS A VISIONARY BLINDED BY
HER VISIONS
URRIOLA alone

If you thought the future was waiting for you down the road,
look back.

I only had one body to bet on life,
and I'm going to lose it anyway.

Dearest night, for you I tip the little I have in my hat,
   futile dreams glowing in the petticoats of space.

For you to look at me with your moonish eye
and silverplate me the way you silverplate the waves.

Watch out

When the chain of the future breaks,
it turns back to when we were beasts.

In a shoe tree

you might find the root
of all beauty.

As if someone swallowed a hundred butterflies
that later slipped out of their mouth and flew far away
like a handkerchief besotted by tears.

Instead of a word, I sheltered a nest of butterfly eggs.

What to do with the stars that still shine,
with the delta waters and the ferries we hid from
so that the tourists wouldn't see two naked women
kissing in the river.

And the sun, what to do with the heat of the sun,
and the crickets, and the eggs of the frogs.

What to do with the miracles of life.

And with the brothel at the port where you laughed
in my arms before taking me to that room where what
was not vanquished by pleasure was seized by forgetfulness.

What to do with farewells,
with suitcases,
with airports,
with elevators,
with sad suits,
with the departure gate,
with the furrow of a cloud,
with the silence of the sky.

There was a time when I delegated my life to god.
Another when I went drinking with the devil.
I tried to play the hero and forgot about myself
to stay alive.

I fought and was defeated,
and I was unfaithful to life,
under various sheets, with death.

I won a few glories only known in the caves
of those who read.
Luminous friends.
Several cats I carry in my memory
and a dog like Unamuno's
whom I freed from writing about my flea-bitten luck.

Of that rise in the river, the reeds, the eggs of the frogs,
the songs of the crickets, and your mouth on me, unbound.

She moves around the room, her steps are slow, like when
you completely forget where you are going.

She approaches a nightstand, runs her fingers along it,
like someone verifying there's stardust on a star.

She goes to the kitchen, puts water in the coffee pot,
fixes her eyes on the gaps that have been loosening
the teeth of the tiles.

A cobweb sways beneath the warm breeze of the water heater.

The coffee boils. She turns off the burner.

She takes out a cup, a cup she does not choose.
She looks at it, confirms it's dawn and that the sun is rising.

She pours the coffee into the coffee cup.

She cannot imagine the landscape that continues
behind the buildings and the hundreds of windows
crammed with people more dead than a cemetery.

She gathers her raincoat and leaves for the café.
To end with you, Prévert.

Et j'ai pleuré

Never fear peace the color of a lizard in the sun

Or the brazenness of waterfalls

Or the paths of the trail

Or a thirst for the shore

Or a night without crickets

Or a forgotten hug

Or a winged back

Or the streets and the criminals

Or the banks and the criminals

Or the useless days

Or the senseless afternoons

Or the pagan nights

Or looking at yourself in the mirror and finding nothing.

A woman wearing a raincoat and high heels crosses the street. Her smooth hand with long fingers grips, the way one firmly clutches the moon, an umbrella made in China.

Her fleeting silhouette is reflected over and over in a puddle of oil and water next to the sidewalk.

I am nothing in her life, only an anonymous witness.

I,   you could   leave.

Poetry, come here beside me, put your hand on my chest
and talk to me about your blind eyes.
The path was never outside, and I've roamed far and wide.
It's been an intense battle watching the sun come up every day,
as if the sun came up.

The night the poet William Osuna read the poem to his mother
while scratching his knee, I remembered Irene.

Irene worked in a brothel in Caracas.
She is 50 years old and as beautiful as death.

In the bathroom she told me she wanted to be a singer.
All that remains of that is a disco ball and a couple of songs
on my lips.

A clock on the wall shaped like the wheel of a ship says it's 4:25.

She is reading Silvia Molloy.
Outside, the train's horn announces a new arrival and
the microbuses exhale a tired whistle. A motorcyclist
bursts in with the deafening sound of a tailpipe that wants
to hightail it.

She returns to the terrace where a bird and I are looking at
each other. She puts her hand on my shoulder.

The only thing I have left of her is the memory of a bird gazing
at me.

I am like a star. Or rather I am like the light
of a dead star that can still travel and touch you
and give you a light I no longer have.

What could I give you that would be more real than my silence?
Because when I speak to you, what I felt when I thought those
words is already gone.

That's why I give you my silence. My silence is everything
I have been. And it's mine.

A poem is neither smaller nor larger than a planet.

A planet that appears and disappears
the way things that travel toward emptiness
appear and disappear.

If you think you are more than dust,
it's just a matter of time.

When you write, you know that you're traveling, that you won't stay long in the same place or with the same people.

When you write, you know that you will be alone in life as often as the road desires it.

When you write, you know that one day you will stop writing.

Then words will have the same meaning as pollen.

Once I wrote so much that I dried up.
I wrote as if I were going to crash head first
into a herd of trains,
as if I were going to fly, as if I could disintegrate me,
integrate me, fear me, and love me.

Once I wrote.

It was a while ago, and I'm sure no one will know
that I wrote as though I were a swarm of poplars.

You may not know it, but trees write,
just sleep under their shade like a *queltehue*
although *queltehue* birds sleep so little like me,
standing upright, leaping.

Because to live is to leap.

If I don't write, the spores of light leave through
the window and don't come back.

That's all I know how to do, wait for words
whose freedom is escape.

Like a storm, you know.

No doubt you've seen it outside, have felt the deafening howl of thunder, have seen it fling fiery bolts to the ground that have split people in two.

Suddenly someone is out in an open field thinking about their problems and is struck by lightning, and the problems disappear. A grazing horse, a paddler in the middle of a canoe on the river, a boat thrashed by the same waves that once rocked it with peaceful happiness.

That's what I have, a storm inside.

I was followed by a twilight dog.
I caressed his mangy head,
because all closeness carries a risk.

He looked at me with the sweetness of those who depart
and have learned to carry all of life with them.

I, who thought I wouldn't have anything, had poetry,
that gave me more lives than a cat,
more waves than a gold picture frame,
more skies than a window.

You appear suddenly one day, in the middle of what used
to be nothing. An immutable summer or winter day,
a lazy afternoon or an irredeemable night.

Suddenly, unexpectedly, like a bird crashing into a window,
you realize that you were a boy and that you ran through life
helter-skelter,
or simply stayed still, watching it silently.

Life will sometimes drag you to the place to which you've always
wanted to return.

This is where I want to be, alone with someone who should
be a Lyrical I and who has no idea what a cup is for.

I want to tell you a story, but it won't be a story you
wind up.
Remember this when you forget me along with all the times
you forget about yourself.
This will be one more reminder.
Remember me when you have nothing to return to
because some things leave no trace.
I say this to you when the leaves crowd the branches,
when the moist shadow of dusk begins to water
the night of Patio 29, where those we search for are missing.

When people dance, their feet move by themselves – even if they don't want them to – they move by themselves.

That song you played on the Wurlitzer at the vacation home reminded me of my father.

My father had lustrous black hair, combed back like his laugh. He wore fashionable suits and trousers with the sharp crease that my mother ironed in, shoes shinier than lightning.

When my father danced, everything was beautiful.
That's why he conquered my mother's heart.
He made her laugh as much as he made her cry.

Of that sorrow and laughter am I made.

On these useless days
in which I prefer to dissent from routine
like a storm cloud,
I feel almost certain
that the rain once reminded you of me.

Being nobody takes some time.
The luminous beauty of youth is the first thing to go,
then fears depart, sorrows, memories, failures.

When you're being nobody there's no room for trivial ruminations.

Being nobody requires that you be it all the time.

I fought forgetfulness, I threw combinations and fake jabs,
I moved my foot and my left hand closer to knock it
off balance.

I sought – the way you seek what you never find –
my opponent's chin.

But forgetfulness knew the exact difference between a jab
and a straight left.

And in a few minutes, I was on the canvas, forgotten.

I was alone and gradually I remained alone.
Like a flower locked in a ball of glass.

I had little because solitude requires little.

I ate alone in countless places and found sweet kisses
in beds I never returned to.

Like a dog without a master, I looked back,
but the scent of the road always wanted me stranded
and empty.

The Instant

Because of an instant when she abandoned me a few decades ago, I found her in the land of horror, open like an air flower, and I made her the home under my feet, my bridge over the abyss, my nonsensical Parnassus, my light, my Lorquian moon, my Hernandian passion, my lover, my Leucadian Rock, my arm raised against life, my spit aimed at heaven, my nomad eye, my sorrow, my laughter, my toasts, my barking at the stars swimming in space, my running in circles, my biting my tail, my regret, my guilt, my smart move, my pencil of sand, my paradise regained, my cemetery, my fleas, my three corners, my shadow, my valley, my path, my gold thimbles, my willow silence, my poplar dance, my heelless shoes, my lame cricket, my maimed butterfly, my gravelly years, my waterfall, my waves, my foam, my shipwrecked boat, my winged fish, my scale, my heart, my nine-pointed star, my peaceful ocean, my whale song, my Southern Cross, my Three Marys, my century of wars and famine, my yearning for a feather in the wind, my sun setting on the shoulder of an elderly woman, my doubt, my deaf and dyslexic experience, my frog in the tree, my stumble, my safety pin, my spoonful of Prévert's coffee, my bells of Apollinaire, my crutch with wheels, my cough, my cigarette, my carousel, my hole without a head, my stampede, my books, my rocks, my useless things, my irony, my creating myself with every word, my privilege, my choice among many to gather a few, my determination, my pleasure, my happiness.

Having found poetry, I didn't devote myself to any master except my verses, nor did I submit to a cacophonous life, nor accumulate grey-suited complaints or the urgencies of ambulances, nor did I stop jumping over fences, nor have the years kept me from embracing trees, nor have the walls of knowledge made it difficult for me to see the sky, nor have I been bewildered by what I see, or by sound, or by composition, nor have I been brave and not written, nor have I been cowardly and stopped writing, nor did I blame anyone for my luck, nor did I think I was a genius or a symbolist prophet, nor did I make a date with anything but transience, nor did I write something unwillingly, nor did I lounge in the comfort of fear, nor was I thwarted by speechlessness or by a few minutes of glory granted by an elite sadder than a thousand mutes, nor was I enthralled by appearances, nor did I win or lose anything that could take me to my grave, nor did I quit or get promoted, nor did I leave or return, nor have I marked my belongings because nothing has belonged to me besides a few instants I've either experienced or read about, nor have I feared rhetorical questions, or the road when it bifurcates, or Tartarus, or Hades, or anguish, or tedium, nor did I sit beauty on my lap in order to denigrate her, nor have I forgotten my nature in spite of the comeliness of its cage.

If I write, it is to navigate the instant, to delay its departure a while longer, fine-tuning the ear of the eye in that brief journey of presence, because every word written and thought in the future will return to the past and vice versa. If I write, it is because the instants wait for me the same way I wait for them. They dwell nearby, on the brink of being named. The object of my desire has been to try – I'm not saying I've ever achieved it – but to try to decipher the mystery of what a full life is to me (as someone who writes, and as my fellow poets must also be a mystery to life). I have conceded the entire import of my existence to the moment of discovery, when poetry emerges before one's eyes, panoptical and blind, and one manages to glimpse its ephemeral presence. In those instants I find myself confronting the understanding, more or less uncertain, and certainly mistaken, of what poetry could even *become*, and what she does with a life when she approaches terrified, made flesh in an instant.

Glass is something that a bird could never imagine.

During the day I write to earn a living
and at night to earn a death.

The way you sometimes leave yourself behind,
the way you find yourself later and forget.

To write is to find and lose yourself at the same time.

We write because life is overwhelming.
It sears us, waterfalls us, engulfs us, liquidates us.

Sometimes it falls a little every day,
even if the sky dislocates a leg and you see its eye,
sometimes closed, sometimes open like a cross-eyed satellite.

What sense does a tree in a pot make,
a mailbox with no letters,
a train track with a rope at the bottom of the sea?

Is there a place where the days that have vanished still live?
Or the things that die, die, the way a fish
falls weightlessly to the bottom, or a robin's heart stops
and the branch can no longer support it.

Why desire anything in a life that is constantly leaving,
like the eyes of flowers when you look at them from inside
a tornado.

Getting lost in space entails frailty for those of us who
float in it.

You say keep your feet firmly on the ground. What ground?
Do you mean this grain of sand that floats at the mercy of frailty?

To be frail is to live with the heart of an air carnation.

A level head is never kept anywhere.

Nowhere is a level head ever really kept.
Although you tilt it like a bird and although you close
your eyelids, although you close them, if you bring it
close, if you seek shelter, if you are drawn to a challenge,
a predicament, a passion, an idea, you will have lost your head over
something.

So where would you ever keep a level head?

I come and go from myself like the wind

What is a poet, if not a hat.

Someone will take us and wear us for a while.
Or we'll have the good fortune to ruin a head of unruly hair.

Someone will throw us off a train of slaves.

Instead, speak to me of gold thimbles and of the journey.
Of that which one day happens like a poem, Diva Plotina
surrounded by asphalt, like an incandescent light in the middle
of mediocrity.

Like the Lion's Claw emerging from the heart of the rock
near Tres Playitas where the ocean speaks to the desert
about thirst.

Speak of the river before they run it dry.
Describe what its wild current was like and what was hushed
by the stones.

I ask you, sea, how not to get carried away or excited,
how to stay calm and not lift the waves even though the wind
pushes me, and how not to beseech the rock or shatter, not kiss
its shore, not drown it at night and retreat in the morning,
how to seem, like you, to belong to everyone and to no one.

I would have wanted to be a tree, to cast down the deepest
roots, to remain alone, clinging to a maddening calm,
even though the wind shook these branches and birds perched on
me, and to support the weight of their bodies, knowing that they
would leave, and not have wanted to fly after any of them
but rather to remain upright and loyal to my shadow.

Where do the days go when they leave?
Under what ray of light can I see their spores depart,
those pale days in which we do not live?

I have drunk from many glasses.

I have taken off my clothes and I have refused to take off
my coat.

So many nights have set me on fire and others have
put me out.

I have no idea why I've loved or stopped loving.

I have no idea why one day or night a strange
coastal dream leads me to the street.

I only know that staying means I stop writing
to devote myself to the affairs of others' lives.

I cannot bear the brevity of life.

I want to write which is exactly the same as living.

Do not come into this house flooded by sorrow
where the night never ends.
The pipes burst and the faucet weeps on the plates,
a lake where the nymphs sing, there's so much water water
that those who rob the rivers envy me.
The sea churns jealously and the moon watches watches me.

Take me to the tallest mountain, my child,
that's where I left this soul snared by thorns.

I have a willow's fear and do not want to be dragged away
by your waters.
This life cannot crash into another rock.

I would like to write you a poem that would shine like
a dying star, leaving a trail of light. Even after
a thousand years, you could watch it die.

When it no longer matters who I was,
except in your memory.
When it no longer matters who you were,
except in my memory.

Never wait for a poem.

Once a poem leaves, it never returns.

To write like someone beginning an ocean journey who has never sailed before, who has never gone deeper than where your feet touch the sand.

I threw myself into an unknown world, and I live not knowing how to swim.

This was perhaps my only brave feat and the most delicious of all my daring deeds.

Do you know what sorrow is?
Look north. Look south. Look at the past and look at the present.
That is sorrow.
We feel sorrow for the *araucaria* trees, for devastation and miserable
ambitions, for the fishermen who share their fish with those who
never had nor ever will have anything. Sorrow for the homeless and
the elderly, for those who have disappeared.

That is the sorrow with which children play,
and dogs and cats get lost
and at the table where tea grew cold, when we thought
that one day sorrow would take
its leave.

I left long before, fumbling in the dark and lost.

I wanted to leave so badly that the day tore me
into two equal parts of fever and farewells.

I was not born to stay in any more lives than mine
or to give you what I wouldn't.

I wear an evening shawl and a spiny solitude.
I can kiss your soul but I would never stay.

What awaits me are the rose bushes, the berries,
the water nymphs, the luck of dogs, the bromeliads,
the sea stars.

I was not born to stay, life of my life.

I am like a star. I can light up your life without you knowing. It doesn't matter if you can't distinguish me from the other stars. It doesn't matter if I am gigantic or so tiny that you could see me shine in the palm of your hand…if you opened it.

The night we danced to Miles Davis's *Ballads and Blues*
the country was falling apart,
and, so as not to cry, we opened a bottle of wine,
and we danced.

They'd sold the country with us inside
and in a few years, we would be their slaves.

Knowing it was the end, we danced.

As when the rivers run dry and sadness seeps and cracks,
and the rocks remain so far from one another

I keep writing things that will turn yellow. I open my eyes
and life goes on, barbaric, medieval, beautiful, and fleeting.

There where the waters sang, they hack the mountains,
cutting off what will never grow again. And thirst?
What will we do about the thirst?

I won't come back, but don't lower your eyelids like the security shutters of the neighborhood hardware store.

I only have the silence of snow.

I no longer wait for anything that is not me.

I is a way of saying that I was – once – my cage and my sky.

Things are made of details. It's the details that make a flower fragile or wild. You might call them thorns. At the other end, they are also wounds. People can, with utter indifference, kill a nocturnal butterfly if they covet its wings or if they are terrified by the radiance of its flight.

Don't look for me where I no longer am, and don't think you know me because I spent time beside you, poetry.

Someone says hello and talks about a business losing money, dogs bark at a young man passing by on a motorcycle, cars carry strangers.
Windows watch over people standing, sitting, or smoking on the balcony of those human niches.

A streetwalker perfumes the light posts and the wires rock gently, throwing an irritable bird off balance.

I do not lose things. Things lose me.
You don't need much to be a wanderer.
The passion of rocks for silence.
Things don't lose me. It's me. I trip like a chair.
One day I leave like a dog following the road.

I'm drawn to the scent of the ocean, to the old tracks of
a train, to the fennel growing under somebody sleeping,
to a rabbit standing upright in the middle of the night,
to rain in a town forgotten
the way we forget the things we love.
Have you listened to Nina Simone?
"Tomorrow is my turn," she sings in a voice fearful
of a life alone.
"Tomorrow is my turn." The tears of birds are dried
by their flight.

I no longer have time to wait for anything that isn't me
because I've lost myself so many times, following someone
or waiting for something. I might say that the times I've lived
intensely were unexpected. When I loved and was loved I didn't
think about it. I threw myself into it the way a rock
throws itself into a fire.

I don't have the heart for anything else

As if I were about to cross a threshold, I get ahead of myself or project and, because I've been condemned to acquiesce, *delete*, I don't acquiesce.

I grow weary and lie down on the legs of the lady.

I'm going to pass through a doorway. Another.
There have been so many.
An umbrella. A thirsty faucet.
That highway that a few years ago was a field of poplars.

Things have changed between yesterday and today.

I am a tree and I'm going out for a walk.

Only the wind would ask where you're from. After blowing
you toward the fog and losing you where the moist bulk of
a dense cloud was everything. Even then, to keep walking in the
emanation that unexpectedly dissipates until we are left alone and
exposed, lost in the light of day.

Like the clouds when they condense into fragments
to later become the sky itself. I know you try to get
my attention, but my attention is volatile. Anything
can distract it, a woman's voice, a child's tears,
a soccer announcer on the radio, the sound of water
slapping the piers of a bridge, or Evans or Baker
or Miles or Alice Coltrane.

A while ago, over the bridge in Boston, I saw the moon
shine as though it had vanquished its reflection in the river.

I am always saying goodbye. I surprise myself leaving.
When people call, I'd like to hang up and return to the silence
that is like coming home.

The death of my mother has left me deaf. That's why
I listen to Beethoven. Sounds we could never imagine
rain down from both.
Do you know the sound of a mother leaving?
A mockingbird sings and her throat inflates, and her
airplane tail is angled, stiff and ready for flight.
She trills things I don't understand. I tilt my head back
and give her a sidelong glance, the same way she looks at me.
She says something pointing to the mountains and disappears
into the air like an armoire. Can it be that a mother who listened
to AM music all day, and sang as much as this mockingbird,
has flown away, and I, who held her in my arms, did not hear
her song or her flight?

I have thrown a rock into the bottom of me.

At the bottom I'm also the rock.

I'm shivering.

I'm wet and I'm shivering.

About the Translator

Elena Barcia is a film and literary translator born and raised in Los Angeles. During her career in the film industry, she translated hundreds of movies from *Hamlet* to *Harry Potter*, and collaborated with directors like Martin Scorsese, Guillermo del Toro, Alfonso Cuarón, and Alejandro Iñárritu on the subtitle translations of their films. Her translation of Miguel de Unamuno's classic novel *Niebla* (*Fog*) was published by Northwestern University Press in 2017. Her poetry translations have appeared in *The Harvard Review, Asymptote, Dark Matter: Women Witnessing, Poetry International,* and *Exchanges, a Journal of Literary Translation.* In both 2020 and 2022 she was a shortlisted for *Poetry International's* Summer Chapbook competition, and her translation of Chilean poet Malú Urriola's *Cadáver exquisito* was published in a bilingual edition by Valparaíso Editions USA in June of 2023. Her anthology of Chilean poet Rosabetty Muñoz's poems titled *Nothing Like Paradise* will be published by Northwestern University Press in 2026.

About the Poet

Malú Urriola (1967-2023) was a Chilean poet, author of seven collections of verse, and the winner of numerous awards, including the Fundación Pablo Neruda's *Premio a la Trayectoria* for her body of work in 2006. Urriola published her first book of poetry, *Piedras rodantes* (*Rolling Stones*; Cuarto Propio) in 1988. Her poems appeared in many anthologies and were translated into English, German, French, and Italian. In addition to her poetry, she wrote scripts for cinema and television and participated in several public multimedia art projects, including *La luz que me ciega* (*The Light that Blinds Me*), featured at the 2015 Venice Biennale. Malú Urriola passed away tragically of pancreatic cancer in July of 2023.

About the Press

Unsolicited Press is based out of Portland, Oregon and focuses on the works of the unsung and underrepresented. As a womxn-owned, all-volunteer small publisher that doesn't worry about profits as much as championing exceptional literature, we have the privilege of partnering with authors skirting the fringes of the lit world. We've worked with emerging and award-winning authors such as Amy Shimshon-Santo, Brook Bhagat, Elisa Carlsen, Tara Stillions Whitehead, and Anne Leigh Parrish.

Learn more at unsolicitedpress.com. Find us on Instagram, X, Facebook, Pinterest, Bsky, Threads, YouTube, and LinkedIn. Unsolicited Press also writes a snarky newsletter on Substack.

www.ingramcontent.com/pod-product-compliance
Lightning Source LLC
Chambersburg PA
CBHW020422130626
46549CB00006B/2695